DATE DUE

12-19-95			
3-11-97			
3-10-98			
5-19-98			
3-10-99			
2-4-00			
11-27-00			
11-13-07			

Demco, Inc. 38-293

Monster
Vehicles

by E.J. Atkinson

Capstone Press
P.O. Box 669, Mankato, MN, U.S.A. 56002-0669

CIP

LIBRARY OF CONGRESS CATALOGING IN PUBLICATION DATA

Atkinson, E. J. (Elizabeth Jane), 1961-
  Monster vehicles / by E. J. Atkinson.
      p. cm. – (Cruisin')
  Summary: Discusses monster trucks, their inventor, and the sport of monster trucking.

  ISBN 1-56065-077-X:
  1. Monster trucks – Juvenile literature. [1. Monster trucks. 2. Trucks.]
  I. Title. II. Series.
  TL230.A85   1989
  629.223 – dc20   89-27866
                                                        CIP
       •   AC

PHOTO CREDITS

Andrew Ryder: 4, 6, 16, 20, 30, 34, 48
Bigfoot: 8, 10, 13, 14, 18, 22, 24, 26, 28, 32, 36, 38, 45, 46

CAPSTONE PRESS
Box 669, Mankato, MN 56001

Contents

Monsters and Trucks

When you think of monsters, you think of big creatures. Monsters seem much stronger and louder than people. Sometimes, monsters can be funny or a little scary. You can think of monster trucks in the same way. A monster truck has huge tires and an engine that ROARS! It climbs over everything in its path. And like the monsters we imagine, monster trucks can be funny or a little scary!

If you like monsters and trucks, then monster trucks will excite you. This book looks at monster trucks. Who invented monster trucks? How are they built? What fun are they and why do people like them?

We will also learn about monster truck safety. It is important to know monster trucking is dangerous. A person must practice a long time to drive a monster truck. Safety is the number one rule.

Who Invented Monster Trucks?

Bob Chandler invented the monster truck. He lives in Hazelwood, Missouri with his wife, Marilyn, and their children. Mr. Chandler is called "the father of monster trucks." Why is he called that? Back in 1974, Mr. Chandler had a blue Ford 4x4 truck. A 4x4 is the short name for a pick-up truck or a **passenger truck** with four-wheel drive. That means the truck has power in all four wheels. Four-wheel drive makes it easier for a truck to drive up hills and through rough places, snow and mud. Most cars have only **two-wheel drive**.

Mr. Chandler's truck was one of the first 4x4s in Hazelwood, Missouri. He learned to fix his truck when it had problems. Other people started to buy 4x4 trucks. They would ask Mr. Chandler to fix their trucks too.

Soon, Mr. Chandler opened a business to fix 4x4 trucks. He called his business Midwest Four-Wheel Drive. The short name is Midwest 4WD and that is still the name today.

Mr. Chandler put his blue Ford truck in front of

Midwest 4WD to attract customers. Little by little, he would add a new part to his truck to make it look fancier. For example, he replaced the old tires with large tires. These tires needed bigger axles. The axle is the bar under a car or truck that holds the wheels and allows them to spin. As you can see, everything on Mr. Chandler's truck grew bigger and bigger. This truck attracted more customers to his business.

Mr. Chandler liked to race his blue 4x4 truck. His friends called him Bigfoot because he put his foot down hard on the gas pedal when he raced. One day, Mr. Chandler painted the name **BIGFOOT** on the side of his truck.

Bigfoot

Bigfoot, the truck, got so big that he had no one to race with. In fact, Bigfoot was heavier and more powerful than any other truck. It became unfair for him to race, because no one could beat him. Instead of competing, Mr. Chandler decided to exhibit Bigfoot. In other words, he went around the country to show everyone his big truck. People paid money to see the famous truck– BIGFOOT, the monster truck. Today, Mr. and Mrs. Chandler own eleven different Bigfoot trucks. Like the first truck, every Bigfoot truck is painted

blue. The trucks travel all over the world to shows during the year.

Other people now build and drive monster trucks. They also perform like Bigfoot. We will take a look at other monster trucks later in the book.

What Is A Monster Truck?

A monster truck is like a 4x4 truck, but has more parts. Each part makes the monster truck look and sound bigger than a regular truck.

Tires: First you notice the huge tires on a monster truck. The tires are usually 5 1/2 feet tall. Sometimes they're even taller. Mr. and Mrs. Chandler's Bigfoot 5 has 10-foot tires. The tires have wide **treads** to help the monster truck grip the track. It's also important that these monster tires have correct tire pressure. That means the tires have the right amount of air.

Engine: The engine in a monster truck must be very powerful. Each engine has between 500 and 700 horsepower. A monster truck engine is five times as powerful as the typical car.

Body: The body of a monster truck is the part you

recognize as a truck. The body is attached to the chassis. That's the frame the body sits on.

Most monster truck bodies are made by regular car companies. Ford and Chevrolet make many of them. A few monster trucks have Dodge bodies. There are also some Japanese-made bodies like Toyota.

Suspension System: Springs lift the body and chassis of the monster truck up off the axle. The springs are also called shock absorbers. When a heavy monster truck drives over a bump, it bounces! The shock absorbers make the bounce feel softer and smoother. A monster truck's shock absorbers can move between 8" and 15" when the tires hit a big bump. This is all part of the suspension system.

Bumpers: Most cars and trucks have bumpers that protect the vehicle when it crashes. Monster trucks have enormous bumpers.

Steering: Did you know that some monster trucks have rear-wheel steering as well as front-wheel steering? By turning the steering wheel you can move the back tires and the front tires. Mr. Chandler was the first person to use rear-wheel steering. Rear-wheel steering helps to turn those big tires more easily.

NISSAN

PLEASE
KEEP
OUT

That's A Monster Truck

Put all these parts and many others on a regular 4x4 truck and you have a monster truck. Owners paint their monster trucks in wild colors and give them funny names. We already met Bigfoot. Other monster truck names are Blue Thunder, Rambo, Stomper, Virginia Giant, and Lone Ranger.

When you put it all together, a typical monster truck weighs between six and eight tons. A ton is equal to 2000 pounds. That means monster trucks weigh between 12,000 and 16,000 pounds. A car weighs between 2000 and 4000 pounds. Monster trucks are about 10 feet high. Each truck costs between $100,000 and $200,000 to make. Some people save money for years to build one monster truck.

Testing is another part of building a monster truck. It has many parts to check over. And drivers want to make sure their trucks run well. Testing can take as long as a month. Once a truck is built and tested, you have to maintain it. In other words, you need to keep fixing it and adding new parts. Maintaining a monster truck can cost as much as $80,000 per year.

Unlike the cars or trucks you see on the road, a

monster truck does not come from a factory in one piece. The owner of a monster truck puts the truck together piece-by-piece. Each part comes from a different factory or, sometimes, the owner builds the part. Every monster truck is one of a kind.

Where Did Monster Trucks Come From?

Monster trucking grew out of many off-road sports. **Off-road** means racing off the paved road, usually on dirt. When did off-road sports begin? After World War II, people started racing the military jeeps left over from wartime. It was fun. Racing jeeps was most popular in the south-western United States in the desert. The races grew so popular they had to be divided into groups. Soon there were all kinds of off-road racing sports.

Some off-road sports are called four-wheeling. That means you drive by yourself or with others off the road in a four-wheel drive truck, car or jeep. There are also off-road races. People drive to one place to compete against each other. Some off-road races include desert racing, hill-climbing, **mud-bogging**, and tractor and truck pulling.

People often connect monster trucking with tractor and truck pulling. In the beginning, monster trucks appeared at tractor and truck pulls to attract more people. Soon, every tractor and truck pull had a monster truck show too. What is a tractor and truck pull? It is an off-road sport that started long ago with horse-pulling.

Where Do Monster Trucks Fit In?

Earlier in the book, we introduced you to Bob Chandler, the father of monster trucks. Mr. Chandler had been pulling and racing with trucks. In the early 1970s, he began to add parts to his blue Ford 4x4 truck. The new truck, Bigfoot, didn't fit into any categories in any races. No other truck was like Bigfoot. So Bigfoot, the monster truck, had no one to compete against.

However, people liked to look at Bigfoot. Mr. Chandler was invited to tractor and truck pulls just to show his monster truck. Then other people started to build monster trucks. They liked the way they looked and roared.

There was one problem. The fans got tired of just looking at the monster trucks. The people who drove monster trucks wanted to do more. Mr. Chandler wondered what was the most exciting thing about Bigfoot. The answer was simple. Bigfoot was strong and loud like a monster. Monsters crushed things and made lots of noise. So Bigfoot learned to act like a monster.

Junk Cars

One day, Mr. Chandler lined up old junk cars in a field. Next, he drove over the top of the junk cars with Bigfoot. All the cars made loud noises and were crushed like cans. Bigfoot bounced around like a giant basketball.

At first, some monster truckers tried competing in the pulls. However, when Mr. Chandler showed other people his car crushing trick, they found it fun to watch. The fans preferred to watch the monster trucks drive over junk cars. So monster trucks stopped pulling and started crushing. By 1980, many people paid money to watch Bigfoot and other monster trucks drive over junk cars.

Monster trucking still takes place at tractor and truck pulls. Now, after the tractor and truck pulling event is over, the monster trucks show up and crush cars.

When the monster trucks drive out into an arena they see junk cars lined up in the middle. Sometimes, the junk cars are stacked on top of each other in **pyramids**. A pyramid is a shape that looks like a tall triangle. Each monster truck drives up and over the junk cars-crushing, banging, and roaring!

Car Crushing

There are few rules to car crushing. The audience chooses the winner. They clap the loudest for the monster truck they like the best. The cars have to be crushed just right.

Where do the cars for the car crush come from? They are rented from a junk yard. The people who are in charge of the show go to a junk yard and pick out lots of old junk cars. They pay about $100 for each car. Then the junk cars are hauled to the show. After the monster trucks crush the cars, the cars are hauled back to the junk yard.

There is no waste when it comes to car crushing. The cars were junk before and they are junk after the show. The crushed cars are still recyclable. That means, the parts and the metal of the car can be used again to build other things.

Beauty Contests

Sometimes, before the car crushing event, there is a beauty contest. The monster trucks drive slowly by the fans. Then the audience claps the loudest for the best looking truck.

Mud-Bogging

Mud-bogging, or mud racing, is another event related to monster trucking. Regular 4x4 trucks compete in mud-bogging. Once in a while monster trucks also enter mud-bogging competitions.

In a mud-bogging race, truckers drive their vehicles as far as they can through deep mud. The truck that drives the farthest wins. This event is funny to watch because mud sprays everywhere. The truck ends up covered in mud. You can see why everyone likes mud-bogging.

Hill Climbing

Hill climbing is another off-road sport. The earlier monster trucks raced in hill climbing events once in a while. Hill climbing is a race that takes place up and over hills. A hill climb can be a short race up a gravel road. It can also be a 12-mile race up a mountain.

The Track

The track is important for all types of competition. Race horses need one type of track, while speed skaters need another. **Pullers**, mud-boggers and monster truckers all need a dirt track. That's one reason why they are called off-road sports.

The track or course takes hours and even days to make. The tractor and truck pulls need a very smooth dirt track. The mud-boggers have up to 200 feet of thick mud. This large area is called a **mud pit**. The monster trucks have more uneven dirt tracks. They drive up and over bumps, jumps and cars. Their tracks are full of surprises.

Indoor tracks are built on top of cement floors. Thousands of pounds of dirt are spread across the floor. Because outdoor tracks are dirt, more dirt is added. Every type of track needs to be maintained during the contest. People shovel and plow the dirt after every **vehicle**.

Safety

You may have guessed that monster trucking is dangerous. The people who drive monster trucks don't want to get hurt either. Half of the money to build a monster truck is spent on safety.

Mr. Chandler is the President of the Monster Trucking Racing Association (MTRA). This group makes sure monster trucking is safe for everyone. Here is a list of items which make monster trucking a safer sport:

- **Rollcage/Rollbar:** If the truck rolls over, a cage and bar around the driver protects him/her.

- **Kill Switch:** If the truck is out of control, a flick of this switch by the driver turns off everything.

- **Harness:** The harness holds the driver in place. It's like a big safety belt in a car.

- **Helmet:** The helmet is a hard hat that protects your head.

- **Kidney Belt:** Your kidneys are important organs in your body. They hurt when you bump a lot. The belt stops your kidneys from getting hurt.

- **Fire Extinguisher:** If your truck catches on fire, the extinguisher puts out the blaze.

- **Engine Shields:** If the engine explodes, the shield holds it in place to protect the driver and people around the truck.

MTRA wants more rules to make monster trucking safer. For example, they want a standard course or track. Today, a monster truck course can be different everytime. That means the driver does not know what the course will look like. If the driver does not know, there is a greater chance something will go wrong. Therefore, one type of course, or a standard course, is safer.

Everyone in monster trucking agrees on one thing. They want excitement with safety. If even one person gets hurt, it is no longer any fun.

The Future of Monster Trucking

Monster trucking keeps changing every year. The trucks are now starting to race one another. Their designs are also changing. And today, monster trucks do not only appear with tractor and truck pulls or other off-road sports. Now, they have their own shows.

Racing

The monster trucks, as you remember, drive up and over junk cars. However, now that's changing. All the fans want to see the monster trucks do more at these events. And the truckers themselves want to try new things.

Lately, monster truck drivers have started to race. They race side-by-side on a flat track. They also race on obstacle courses. An **obstacle course** is a track with different things to drive around. For example, the driver may have to go up and around a barrel. Sometimes, they even race over the junk cars. Racing is exciting and difficult.

A driver needs speed to race side-by-side on an obstacle course. In both cases, the fastest truck wins.

New Design: Fiberglass

Now that monster trucks are racing, changes are being made. The truck parts are lighter, and the body is made from fiberglass. Fiberglass is strong, yet lightweight, material used to make a variety of things. For example, boats and fishing rods are often made of fiberglass. Monster trucks, as we said before, weigh between six and eight tons. The new fiberglass monster trucks will weigh between four and five tons. The lighter they are, the faster they will go.

Monster Trucks Only

For a long time, monster trucks have been showing up at other off-road sports events. The most common sporting event where you see monster trucks is tractor and truck pulling. Now monster trucks have many fans who want to see only monster trucking. Since monster trucks race each other as well as crush cars, they can entertain the crowds for hours.

Meet Some Monster Truckers

Everett Jasmer owns a famous Chevy monster truck called USA-1. Mr. Jasmer is glad to see monster trucks race now. He felt car crushing was boring. USA-1 is lighter than most monster trucks. Mr. Jasmer knows it is important to keep a truck light and powerful to win races.

Jeff Bainter and Debbie Rhoden own monster jeeps. The body of their monster truck is a real jeep body. The first monster jeep they built was named Hot Stuff. Now they own another jeep named High Voltage. High Voltage is lighter and faster than Hot Stuff. Hot Stuff is a strong car crusher and High Voltage is a fast racer.

Bob Chandler, owner of the eleven Bigfoots, has tried something different. His tenth Bigfoot is named Fastrax. Fastrax is a van built on top of rolling army tank tracks. Instead of regular tires, Fastrax climbs over and around on army tank tracks.

You may think only men drive monster trucks. That is not true. Women, like Debbie Rhoden, are

entering the contests more and more. Marilyn Chandler was the first woman to drive a monster truck. Many women also attend the big events.

Fun Facts

- Do you know how to climb into a monster truck? It isn't easy. If a truck is ten feet high you can't just hop in. You need to climb up on the tire and over to the step on the cab. Then pull yourself through the door.

- Do you know how to get a monster truck from one city to another? You need a special trailer to put the monster truck in. Then you pull the trailer with a regular truck.

- Monster trucks have extra parts to excite the crowds. Some monster trucks have flashing lights. Others can raise their hoods up and down. Some have loud and funny honking horns. Everything makes the show exciting to watch.

- Monster trucks need many people to take care of them during contests. The people who do this are called the **pit crew**. For example, if a piece in the engine breaks, the pit crew fixes it as fast as they can. The pit crew is an important part of monster trucking.

- Did you know that monster trucks have been invited to perform as far away as Japan? People all over the world like to watch the trucks with the big tires.

- In September,1989 Bob Chandler gathered all eleven Bigfoots for the first time in one place. The reason was to celebrate the 5000th showing of all the Bigfoot trucks.

- Did you know that monster trucks float? A car sinks in the water, but not a monster truck. If you drive one into the water, the air in the big tires keep it floating along.

- The largest crowd at a monster truck event was 72,000 people. This happened at the Silverdome in Pontiac, Michigan.

Bigfoot International Fan Club

If you want to join the Bigfoot International Fan Club and have your parents permission, write to:

Bigfoot International Fan Club
6311 North Lindbergh Blvd.
Hazelwood, MO. 63042

They will write back and tell you how to join. If you do join, you will receive a kit which includes:

- An official membership card
- Stickers
- A folder
- An 8"x10" Photograph

The Club will send you a newsletter with monster truck news twice a year. The best part is the birthday surprise. On your birthday, you will receive a monster truck surprise.

Allow four to six weeks for your kit to arrive. The people in Hazelwood need the following information from you:

Your Name

Your Address/City/State/Zip Code

Your Age

Your Birthday (for the Birthday   Surprise)

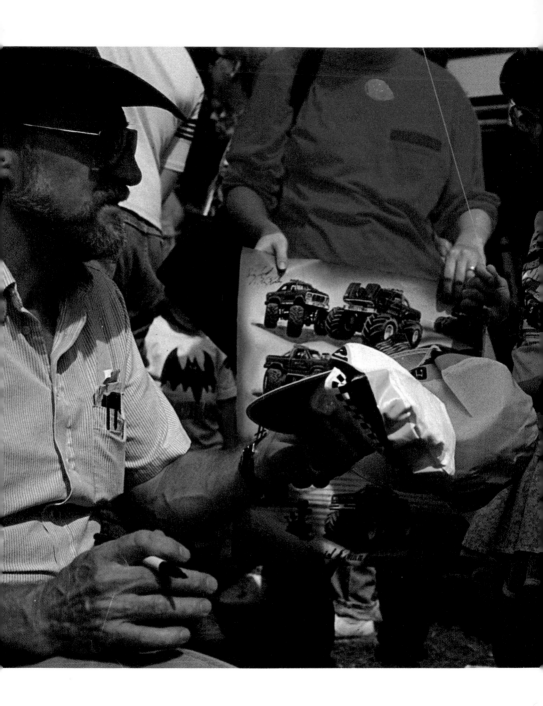

The Father of Monster Trucks

An Interview with Bob Chandler

I talked with Bob Chandler about his Bigfoot trucks. He was happy to tell me about the sport of monster trucking and how it began.

What were you doing before you built Bigfoot 1?

I was a carpenter. Then I bought the first 4x4 truck in the area. I learned how to fix it myself. Other people started buying 4x4 trucks. They asked me to work on them. That's how I started my business, Midwest 4WD. Today I own Midwest 4WD and Bigfoot 4x4, Inc.

When was Bigfoot 1 started and finished?

I started working on my Ford 4x4 truck in 1974. I added parts and changed things a lot. The final Bigfoot 1 you see today was finished in 1982. It took eight years altogether.

When did monster trucking as a sport begin?

I believe it began in 1982 when we used the 5 1\2 foot tires and Bigfoot 1 was finished.

Where do you get those big tires for your monster trucks?

The tires come from special farm machines. They are called **terra tires**. These tires can drive on a farm and not hurt the land. They move very softly on the ground, yet they are very big.

How fast does your fastest monster truck go?

My fastest truck is Bigfoot 1. It can go as fast as 130 m.p.h. I never drive it faster than 50 m.p.h.

How many cars have you crushed at one time?

I crushed fifty cars at once for a television program called, THAT'S INCREDIBLE. That was in 1983, I believe, and I used Bigfoot 2.

How old do you have to be to drive a monster truck in competition?

You must be eighteen years old.

Who are some of your toughest competitors?

I would say Gravedigger and Carolina Crusher. Carolina Crusher is one of the best, because he is consistent. That means he is always the same. The truck is driven well–not too fast and with skill. He also races every weekend. To win you must be consistent, not the fastest or most powerful.

How many miles to the gallon does a monster truck get?

I think about 1 mile to the gallon.

Do you have children? If so, are they monster truckers?

Yes, I have three children. Bobby, Penny, and Ann.

All of my children have driven the trucks. They go to events and help with the business. I don't know if they want to be full-time drivers or monster truckers.

Can kids visit the monster trucks after an event?

Sometimes they can. That depends on the rules of where the event takes place. For example, in Madison Square Garden (in New York City), they can't let all those people come down off the stands and onto the floor. But at small fairs, people can look at the trucks up close and ask questions.

About your safety group, Monster Truck Racing Association, what are you doing about safety right now?

One thing we want to do is make a restriction on the size of the engine. That means, make a rule that says the engine can be only this big. The reason is, some people put engines in their trucks that are too big. That makes the truck hard to control, which isn't safe.

Another thing we are trying to do is make a special driver's license. Right now, anyone who drives trucks can drive a monster truck. We think people should learn more about monster trucks first and then take a test. If they pass the test they get a special driver's license to compete.

Is the Bigfoot International Fan Club popular?

It sure is. We have over 20,000 members.

What are the names of all your Bigfoot trucks?

Okay, here it goes: **1)** Bigfoot 1 was completed in 1982. **2)** Bigfoot 2 was completed in 1982. **3)** Bigfoot 3 was completed in 1983. **4)** Bigfoot 4 was completed in 1984. **5)** Bigfoot Ranger was completed in 1985. **6)** Bigfoot Shuttle was completed in 1985. **7)** Bigfoot 5 was built in 1986. **8)** Bigfoot 6 was completed in 1986. **9)** Bigfoot 7 was completed in 1988. **10)** Bigfoot Fastrax was completed in 1988. **11)** Bigfoot 8 was completed in 1989.

How long do you test a new truck?

I test each of my trucks 30 to 40 days before they show before the public.

In what way is Bigfoot 8 different from the other trucks?

Bigfoot 8 is very different. The truck has a totally tubular frame like a drag racing car. It looks like a dune buggy on giant wheels. The truck is all one piece and made from fiberglass. The fiberglass makes it light but strong.

 Most of my trucks weigh about 7 tons. This one will weigh only 5 tons. It also has 24" suspension. That means it will ride very high off the wheels.

What do other people think of Bigfoot 8?

I believe Bigfoot 8 will change monster trucking completely. The new tubular design and fiberglass is the way monster trucks will look in the future. Do you know I designed it on my computer?

Do you still drive your trucks?

Yes, I do, but Jim Kramer is my best driver. He is also the Vice President of Bigfoot 4x4, Inc. I spend my time designing and building the trucks.

How many shows a year do your trucks appear in?

We appear in over 600 shows a year. We go to Australia, Hong Kong, Japan, and South America, to name a few places. We have appeared in every state in the United States including Hawaii, Alaska and Puerto Rico.

How do you get a Monster truck to Australia

We haul it to the west coast and put it in a large carton. Then it is sent on a ship to Australia. It takes 1 to 1 1/2 months to travel each way.

Can people stop at Midwest 4WD to see the trucks?

Please do stop and visit us. We are in Hazel-wood,Missouri off of Highway 270 on Lindbergh Boulevard. I leave Bigfoot 5 on display out front. That is the truck with 10-foot-tires. I also put other Bigfoot trucks out for people to see if they are not being repaired.

Do you give tours?

We always give the kids a tour if we have time. We also have a store full of souvenirs.

Your Bigfoot trucks have been in movies, cartoons and in parades. What else have your trucks done?

Bigfoot trucks have been in six movies. We have also been on television many times. My wife, Marilyn, appeared on the Public Television Show, 3-2-1 CONTACT, talking about the tires.

We also help out as much as we can with charities. We often work with the Make-A-Wish program.

Children who are very sick and who are part of Make-A-Wish sometimes visit Bigfoot. We take them for a special drive.

That's nice of you to give your time to charities. You must be a very busy person.

Yes, Marilyn and I want the Bigfoot trucks to be good guys and not bad guys. They can help a lot. For example, they have been in anti-drug videos telling kids to "Just Say No." We will never allow beer or tobacco companies to paint their names on our trucks. We want to help children have fun.

Why do you like the sport of monster trucking?

I really like monster trucking because I meet a lot of people and because the kids love the trucks. I love to do a race and watch the kids laugh and smile. I don't know why the kids like them so much, but they do!

Glossary

Mud Bogging – An off-road sport which involves racing mostly 4x4 trucks through a mud pit.

Mud Pit – A deep or large area filled with mud. A mud pit is used in the off-road sport of mud-bogging.

Obstacle Course – A track or path with objects that stand in the way. In competition, the driver travels around and over the objects.

Off-Road – This refers to off-road sports that take place off the paved road.

Passenger Truck – A two-wheel or four-wheel truck used for everyday use, like a pick-up truck or 4x4.

Pit Crew – The people who take care of a vehicle during competition.

Puller – The driver who competes in a tractor or truck pull.

Pyramid – A shape that looks like a standing triangle.

Terra Tires – Special tires from farm equipment used on many monster trucks.

Treads – The deep tracks in a tire which help it to grip the road.

Two -Wheel Drive – A vehicle with power in two out of four wheels has two-wheel drive. Most cars have two-wheel drive.

Vehicle – Any machine that carries or transports something or someone. Examples: bicycle, car, train, truck.